PHP in 123

Nick Mendoza

FortBend HOST
FortBendHost.com

PHP in 123

Printed in the United States of America

ISBN: 1494719320

ISBN-13: 978-1494719326

www.FortBendHost.com

DEDICATION

This book is dedicated to my Mother; for teaching me to think outside the box and to always finish what I start. Your love, sacrifice, and hard work made me the person that I am today.

CONTENTS

ACKNOWLEDGMENTS

I would like to express my great appreciation to Sarah Mendoza from SEEM Photography for the back cover photo and for help with the title. I would also like to thank NASA for the use of their image on the cover. Special thanks to Brent Leger for the encouragement and helping me roll with a few ideas.

1 INTRODUCTION

Learning a programming language does not require a high IQ. Nor does it require a college degree or advanced mathematics. It only requires your patience, consistency, and a desire to learn. *Patience*, in that you must be willing to search for the answers that you need. You will learn a lot by stretching past your comfort level and trying to figure out how to implement the functionality that you want to add to your scripts. *Consistency*, in that you must be able to devote some time everyday to learning and improving your skills (especially in the beginning). *Desire*, in that new material is uncomfortable to learn. If this is your first programming language, some aspects may initially seem a little confusing. It's nothing that you cannot handle, but it will be a lot less fun than watching television.

I won't spend much time trying to convince you why you should learn PHP. If you're browsing through this book, then you probably already understand its importance. With the rise in popularity of CMS platforms written in PHP, like Wordpress, Drupal, or Joomla, it is more popular than ever. While it is nice to understand how these frameworks function down the line, right now learning the basics is the goal. A very important aspect of learning any programming language is having an abstract view of how the language works. Once you understand the basics, through practice you'll, be able to apply those basics and come to your own conclusions on how to solve problems. This book is geared towards that approach.

Who should read this book?

Anybody that is new to PHP should read this book. I have made every attempt to skip what you don't need to know and instead get right to the point. You don't need to know how the binary that lets you interpret PHP is compiled, but I will tell you that PHP is an interpreted language. You may want to learn all of that later, but you don't need to know it to get an enormous amount of use out of PHP. This also means that you should not skip any chapters. Even if you feel like you already understand the material, read it anyway. You may pick up tidbits of information that you didn't know about and find it useful down the line.

Why should you listen to me?

I hold a Bachelor's Degree in Computer Science and have worked as a PHP developer for many years. I learned a lot pursuing my degree, but I've also worked for bosses that held no degree at all; they simply learned what they needed to about coding and set out to build a product that people wanted. This is what I direct you to do. As such, I will walk you from learning about what variables are, all the way up to writing scripts. Whether you decide to work for yourself or for a company, your value (and income) will be a result of what you can produce.

What do you need?

You will need a webhosting account with a public IP address and PHP already installed. The LAMP solution stack (Linux, Apache, MySQL, and PHP) is your best bet since it generally has the lowest cost. You will also need a text editor (VIM or NotePad++ is preferred). If you don't have any of that available or aren't sure how to set it up yourself, I've created a special package for my readers that will make everything that you need available at a low price. Please visit this link to find out more:

http://FortBendHost.com/Book-Offer

Final words before we start:

With so much media coming at us all from every angle, it can be difficult to focus. People's attention spans have become very short and most people that start this book will never even come close to finishing. While it is unfortunate for them, it is fortunate for you. People with moderate to long attention spans have a wealth of information at their fingertips like never before. PHP has one of the best online documentation libraries out there and almost every common problem has been documented on some level. Most solutions can be found by simply pasting your error message into a search engine, which may have previously taken you hours in debugging time.

2 OVERVIEW

Since PHP is a server-side scripting language (the server processes it before serving it to the user), you will see it mostly being used as the engine for websites. However, the main building block of the web is HTML. HTML consists of opening and closing tags which format a page's layout:

```
<!DOCTYPE html>
<html>
  <head>
    <title>Title goes here</title>
  </head>
  <body>
    Page content goes here.
  </body>
</html>
```

HTML was created to control the flow of a webpage, but it was not designed to look good.

Cascading style sheets (CSS) were added and made it much easier to edit and add styles to HTML with divisors and classes. As useful as they are, HTML and CSS are not dynamic. They cannot be tailored to effectively personalize pages. This is where a server-side scripting language (like PHP) comes in. Did you ever wonder how shopping carts or *recommended* pages worked? Code on the back end syncs all of that and gives you a personalized experience. So when you visit a website, the main page could be a PHP script that runs, probably connects to a database to retrieve some information, processes the information, then outputs a custom-tailored HTML response back to the user.

There is one more fundamental piece to the puzzle, which allows websites to act more like desktop applications with their immediate responsiveness. That is a client-side scripting language like **Javascript** or **Actionscript**. It is called client-side, because it is not parsed by the server. Instead, the code (in one form or another) is downloaded and parsed by the user's browser. You may be wondering why there is both a client-side and a server-side need for code. The reason is because once the server has processed the code, it disconnects and loses its state. The client-side script can allow polling or a reconnection at certain intervals or upon certain actions to send or receive requests. This allows a lot of functionality, like drag and drop portions of a page or a chat script. It also saves bandwidth by validating information before it is sent to the server. However, you should never send sensitive data to the client. Make sure that sensitive data is processed by the server-side scripting language (like database usernames and passwords).

That is the general flow. HTML and CSS are static portions that make up a webpage, PHP handles processing on the server-side, and any client-side scripting language will be downloaded by the user and parsed via their browser. This book focuses on PHP, the server-side scripting language.

It is extremely important that you grasp all of this, as it is the most abstract view of how things work. If you are unclear about anything, please re-read this chapter.

3 PHP BASICS

This chapter will cover the general layout of PHP, data types (variables), how to change/cast them, and how to comment your code.

PHP is a recursive acronym that stands for *PHP: Hypertext Preprocessor.* It used to stand for *Personal Home Page* back when it was created years ago, but changed with the release of PHP 3.

PHP script file names should end with ".php". For example, the main page on your website will be *index.php* (other file setups *can* be configured, but this is the general formula). Inside the script, blocks of code should begin and end with PHP tags:

```php
<?php
# Code goes here.
?>
```

<?php is the preferred opening tag, as it is the most system compatible (common) method, but other tag options exist that are not recommended. These include short tags:

```
<?
# Code goes here.
?>
```

as well as ASP tags, which are not enabled by default on most servers:

```
<%
# Code goes here.
%>
```

ASP (Active Server Pages) is a separate server-side scripting language which was developed by Microsoft, so there is no sense in mixing it with PHP. Simply use <?php ?> to wrap all of your code (standard tags).

Let's look at a script called *index.php* and work through what all of the elements mean:

```
<?php

/**
 * This is a DocBlock.
 */

# Single line comment.
// Also a single line comment.

echo "Hello World\n";
```

```php
echo 'Hello World\n';

?>
```

We start with our opening <?php tag. This tells us that PHP is about to follow. Next we have a *DocBlock*. This is a special type of comment that may span multiple lines. Anything between /* and */ will be skipped over by PHP. Programmers tend to use *DocBlocks* to explain what the lines of code about to follow actually do. Comments are completely skipped by PHP and are essentially notes that you leave yourself. For single line comments, PHP supports # (script style) and // (C++ style) comments. These can only span one line.

echo is a language construct and allows you to output to standard output (stdout). Another one that you're likely to come across is *print,* but for our purposes, consider it to perform the same function as *echo*. The *string* of text that follows is shown first in double quotes, then in single quotes. Double quotes are interpolated, meaning that the information in them is parsed before being displayed. Single quotes are literal and do no interpolating. In our case, the first example will output *Hello World* and then the *\n* (special character) is interpolated to send us a newline (jump to the next line). In the single quote case, since nothing is interpolated, we will see *Hello World\n*. There is a third method called heredoc syntax (interpolated), but it is far less commonly used than double quotes and will be skipped.

PHP statements, or lines of execution, must end with a semicolon. You'll notice that each *echo* command has one. This tells PHP that this is the end of your command. Whitespaces (spacebar, tabs, and the like) are also skipped over by PHP. These two examples will display exactly the same on screen:

```
echo      "Hello World\n"    ;
echo "Hello World\n";
```

Similarly, while it is good form to only put one command per line, PHP will allow you to put as many as you like, so long as they are properly terminated with the semicolon:

```
echo "Hello World\n"; echo 'Hello World\n';
```

Again, it's best to only put one command per line due to readability. Also, only use as many whitespaces as you need to make readability easier.

PHP is a weakly typed programming language. In general terms, this means that variables can be referenced or assigned without actually existing. While this may sound great, it can create a lot of debugging work if you're not careful planning and writing your code. This brings us to *variables*, which are dynamic values that are stored and manipulated. They are also *case sensitive*. Being that PHP allows the web to be dynamic, it is essential that variables exist. They allow us to store names, numbers, etc and act as containers. Variables begin with a dollar sign and continue with the variable name (no whitespaces). They can store all types of values:

```
$num = 1; # Integer
$dec = 1.5; # Float (or decimal)
$lies = false; # Boolean (true/false)
```

```php
$name = "Nick"; # A string of characters
$list = array(); # Arrangement of values
```

Variables should be named in a way that is descriptive and easy to read. A common solution is to use the *camel case* method. This just means that if the variable name is more than one word, the first letter of the first word is lowercase, then each word after that has its first letter in uppercase:

```php
$prodCost = 10;
$localTax = 5;

$totalCost = $prodCost + $localTax;
```

In the spirit of PHP being weakly typed, any value may be referenced at any time, but if it was not declared, it will be NULL. NULL is a special type that is essentially no type. It is simply no value at all. You can also manually make a value null by assigning it as such:

```php
$val = NULL;
```

Being weakly typed, a variable can also be re-declared as another variable further down the line:

```php
$val = 1;
$val = "a string";
$val = 1.5;
```

A *boolean* value is the most primitive that you will come across. It simply has a value of *true* or *false*. The number 1 and 0 will also translate to true and false, respectively, when strict variable types are not checked (explained later). Booleans are useful for checking whether a function was successful or not.

Arrays are the most complicated of all of the variables types that we've covered so far, but they are extremely powerful in PHP. An array acts as a container that can store many types of different variables (even more arrays themselves) and are associated with keys. If you don't declare any keys, the array will simply use keys that start from number 0 and move up one per index. You may also use *associative* keys which allow keys to be other than numeric, and they may be mixed with numeric keys as well. Let's take a look at a basic array:

```php
<?php

# Declare an empty array:
$arr = array();

# Declare an array with numeric keys:
$arr = array("1", "2", "3");

# Now let's add some values:
# Pushes a value onto the end.
$arr[] = "4";
# Pushes a value onto the end.
$arr[] = "100";

# Create an associative array:
$arr = array("name" => "Nick",
             "0" => "value");

?>
```

An array that has no values in between the parenthesis is empty by default. However, later on, the array is re-declared to store the values 1, 2, and 3. The number *1* is stored at index 0, *2* at index 1, and *3* at index 2. If you were to output the result, it would look like this:

Array
(
   [0] => 1
   [1] => 2
   [2] => 3
)

You'll notice that on the next few lines, we push the number "4" onto the end of the array (with the []) and we also do the same with the number "100". This gives us the result:

Array
(
   [0] => 1
   [1] => 2
   [2] => 3
   [3] => 4
   [4] => 100
)

The [] operation (open/close square brackets) simply pushes the assigned value onto the end of the array. The command following that overwrites the value that we made and declares an associative array. You'll notice that there is a difference as to how the array values are assigned. The "=>" operator assignes a key to a name (key => name). The result that we end with is:

Array
(
   [name] => Nick
   [0] => value
)

Assigning the key/value pair would have worked exactly the same with our first array by simply setting the key to be the number that we wanted assigned:

```
$arr = array("0" => "1",
             "1" => "2", "2" => "3");
```

However, that would have been more work to write and would have given us the exact same result.

   You may access array elements (indexes) by directly referencing the value and index. Let's look at our array:

```
$arr = array("1", "2", "3");

# Change a value:
$arr[0] = "Hello";
```

After the declaration, we have:

Array
(
   [0] => 1
   [1] => 2
   [2] => 3
)

Once the value is changed, we have:

```
Array
(
    [0] => Hello
    [1] => 2
    [2] => 3
)
```

This also applies to associative arrays, which have an index name that you assign. In our earlier case, the value would have been $arr["name"] = "Hello";

Another very important data type is the *string*. A string is simply a set of characters grouped together. You've seen them a few times throughout this book in the forms:

```
# Simple strings:
$val = "a string";
$name = "Nick";

# Array element as a string.
$arr[0] = "Hello";
```

Strings may have spaces within their values. They may also contain other variables within their values. Jumping back to interpolated strings (double quotes), this is allowed:

```
$var = "some value";
$str = "This is $var";
# This will output:
# This is some value
echo $str;
```

Single quoted strings would output a literal value and would not interpolate anything:

```
$var = "some value";
$str = 'This is $var';

# This will output:
# This is $var
echo $str;
```

Strings may also be put together, or *concatenated*. The concatenation operator in PHP is the period ("."). Think of concatenation like glue, where you glue pieces together:

```
$var1 = "Hello";
$var2 = "World";

// This will output:
// Hello World
echo $var1 . " " . $var2;
```

We declare $var1 to be a string containing the value "Hello". $var2 is declared and assigned the string "World". We then use echo to print the message to stdout (standard output), and we concatenate a space as " ".

The last two data types that we will cover for this chapter are *integers* and *floating point numbers (floats)*. *Ints* and *floats* are numeric. You can add, subtract, multiply, divide, etc, and the value stored will vary on what type of system you run PHP on. Generally, ints can store a value up to 2 billion (It is important to remember that when performing math on an int). *You should never perform math on a float.* Accuracy on a float is not usually very good. Unless you're simply rounding a number, math should be performed only on ints, then the decimal place moved for printing sake only.

```
# Integer:
$num = 1;

# Float:
$num2 = 1.5;
```

If you ever need to change the type of value that is represented, you simply have to *cast* it to the desired variable type:

```
$num = 1.2;

// $newNum becomes 1
$newNum = (int)$num;
```

Casting a float to an int drops the decimal. Casting a variable that does not exist to an int will assign a 0. Casting a variable that does not exist to a string will result in an empty string:

```
// $val will be empty
$val = (string)$DoesNotExist;

// $num will be 0
$num = (int)$nothing;
```

In this chapter you learned about the general layout of PHP, data types (variables), casting, and how to comment your code. If you feel confused about any of this, please read this short chapter again. Then proceed to the next chapter to learn how to manipulate data to get useful output.

4 MANIPULATING DATA

Now that you've learned about different data types and the general layout of PHP, it's time to learn how to manipulate data to get what you need from PHP. Let's start by taking a look at *ints* again. There are many different ways to add, subtract, multiply, and divide numbers:

```php
# Our integer values:
$val = 5;
$val2 = 5;

$val = $val + 1;
# Now $val equals 6.

$val2 += 1;
# $val2 also equals 6.

$total = $val + $val2;
# $total equals 12.
```

First we declare $val and $val2, assign them equal values, then run the same operations on them, just in different ways. We perform our operation on $val2 using what's called the *addition assignment* operator, which is shorthand for running the same execution as we did on $val. It is important to note that during assignment, the right hand side of the equation is assigned to the left hand side. The operation on $val2 simply illustrates in shorthand that you must assign to the left hand side the result of the left hand side *plus* the right hand side. We can perform the exact same operation type using multiplication, division, and even string concatenation:

```
# Our integer values:
$val = 5;
$val2 = 5;

$val = $val - 1;
$val2 -= 1;
# Both equal 4.

$val = $val * 2;
$val2 *= 2;
# Both equal 8.

$val = $val / 2;
$val2 /= 2;
# Both equal 4.

$val = $val % 3;
$val2 %= 3;
# Both equal 1.
```

```
$val = "Some text";
$val2 = "Some text";

$val = $val . " is going to be output";
$val2 .= " is going to be output";
# Both hold the same string value.
```

One operator that you haven't seen mentioned here before is the *modulus* (%). This operator works similar to divide, but instead of saving the result, it saves the remainder. So when 4 is divided by 3, it will divide once and leave a remainder of 1. If you divide 4 by 2, it will divide twice, leaving us a remainder of 0. The modulus is the *remainder* value.

Multiple operations can also be performed within the same statement. The order of operations is the same as it is when using math, which is multiplication and division are performed left to right, then addition and subtraction are left to right. However, just like in math, the order of operations can be changed when parenthesis are used:

```
# Mult and division, left to right.
# Then add and subtract, left to right.
$x = 5 * 2 + 6 / 3 - 1;
# $x equals 11.

# The order of operations has changed,
# which gives us a different answer:
$x = 5 * 2 + 6 / (3 - 1);
# $x equals 13.
```

You may also nest as many parenthesis as you see fit for your purpose.

Since addition and subtraction are so popular in programming due to conditional looping (covered later), there are even shorter ways to add and subtract numbers:

```
$i = 1;

$i++;
# $i now equals 2.
++$i;
# $i now equals 3.

$i--;
# $i now equals 2.
--$i;
# $i now equals 1.
```

Using ++ or – simply says *add 1 to our value*, or *subtract 1 from our value* (respectively). You'll notice that the operators sometimes show up before the variable name, and sometimes they show up after the variable name. This is because during certain conditions (covered later in this chapter), you may want to evaluate the result of your operation *before* or *after* the result has been saved.

There will also be times when you don't want to hard code a value to a variable, but rather you need it to be dynamically assigned.

```
$var = "Some text";
$x = $var;
# Both have the same value now.
```

In all of the cases shown so far, we have simply made a copy of a variable when assigning the value to another variable. However, there is a way to have a value reference the original instead of merely copy it. You may use the reference operator (&) to reference another variable. As a result, any changes made to either affect both variables:

```php
$first = "This is ";
$second = " a string";

echo $first . $second;
# Outputs "This is a string".

# '&' is the reference operator.
$first = &$second;
$second = "Updated string";

echo $first;
# Outputs 'Updated string'.
echo $second;
# Outputs 'Updated string'.

$second = "Last string";

echo $first;
# Outputs 'Last string'.
echo $second;
# Outputs 'Last string'.

unset($first);
# Reference killed.
```

Keep in mind that references in PHP are not like pointers in the C programming language. In PHP they are only symbol table aliases. Generally, you will not need to reference variables, but rather you'll want to assign them like we've shown previously.

There may be some instances where you'll need to store a variable name for a variable. It isn't used too often and I recommended it be used sparingly (if at all), but there are times where you may not know what the name of a variable may be. For this case, there are *variable variables*. Variable variables are best explained by example:

```php
$var = "my";
$$var = " variable variable";
# $$var first parses $var,
# so it's the same as setting '$my'

$output = $var . $$var;

echo $output;
# Outputs 'my variable variable'
```

The above example may look a little confusing, so let's walk through it. As you've seen many times, we first assign the string "my" to $var. Next, we save whatever the value of $var is as the name of our variable variable. This allows us to make a truly dynamic variable name. We assign the string " variable variable" to the value of $$var (which is just $my). Then we concatenate both strings and output the result. And that's it! However, I recommended that you rarely use this method, as it can cause you much angst when it's time to debug your code.

You've learned how to manipulate data in this chapter. Since each chapter builds upon what you've learned in the previous chapter (just like math), make sure that you understand everything before moving on. In the next chapter we'll learn about *control structures*.

5 CONTROL STRUCTURES

Now that you can manipulate data in PHP, the next step is learning about *flow control*. Flow control lets you decide when you want specific events to occur. The most common is the *if/else* condition. An if statement may exist on its own, without an else, but not vice versa. Let's look at some sample code:

```php
# Set our boolean:
$jumpIn = true;

if ($jumpIn) {
    echo "We jumped in!";
} else {
    echo "We skipped it.";
}

# Outputs 'We jumped in!'
```

The *if* part of our code evaluates the condition to be true or false. In the above example, we hard code a boolean value to be *true*, then we evaluate it. If the boolean value had been *false*, the condition would not have been met and we would have jumped to our *else* statement.

It's important to always use an opening curly brace after the expression and a closing curly brace at the end of the code block. All of the code within the curly braces will fall under the condition that precedes it. Otherwise, only the first statement after the condition will fall under that condition (remember that comments are, however, completely ignored):

```
$var = false;

if ($var) {
    echo "Yay!\n";
    echo "We're inside!";
}

# Outputs nothing at all.
```

Otherwise, without curly braces, we get an undesired result:

```
$var = false;

if ($var)
    echo "Yay!\n";
    echo "We're inside!";

# Outputs: "We're inside!"
```

The *else if* statement allows even more flexibility. The else if must follow an *if* statement or another *else if* statement and cannot exist on its own:

```php
$var = true;

if ($var) {
    echo "true!";
} else if (!$var) {
    echo "false!";
} else {
    echo "Where are we?";
}
```

So we check to see if our first condition (if) is true. If it is not, then we check if our second condition (else if) is true. If it is not, then we default to our else statement. Again, you're not restricted to one if/else statement. You can have any combination of statements, including nested ones:

```php
$var = true;

if ($var) {
    if (!$var) {
        echo "Hello!";
    } else {
        echo "Bye!";
    }
} else {
    echo "It's false!";
}
```

You'll notice that in our else if condition we put an exclamation point to the left of the variable, inside parenthesis. This *logical operator* simply tells give us the opposite of what our result is (*true* becomes *false* and vice versa). This is very useful for checking conditions, but it isn't enough to make conditions extremely useful. These are where *comparison operators* come in. If you have 2 variables that change depending on user input, you can compare them and then follow the condition that suits your needs:

- \> (greater than)
- \< (less than)
- \>= (greater than or equal to)
- \<= (less than or equal to)
- != (does not equal)
- == (is equal to in value)
- === (is identical to in type and value)

Let's look at an example:

```
$val = 5;
$val2 = 6;
if ($val >= $val2) {
    if ($val > $val2) {
        echo "It's greater than!";
    }
} else if ($val <= $val2) {
    if ($val < $val2) {
        echo "It's less than!";
    }
} else if ($val != $val2) {
    echo "They are not equal.";
} else if ($val == $val2) {
```

```
    if ($val === $val2) {
        echo "They are identical!";
    }
}
```

As you can see, comparison operators give us a lot of flexibility. Remember, the result of the operation within the parenthesis for the if statement is what decides whether it will be executed or not. *True* means execute and *false* does not.

Writing a lot of if/else statements can get pretty tedious, especially if there are a lot of cases to check for. The *switch* statement is much less commonly used, but can be very useful:

```
$val = 2;

switch ($val) {
    case 0:
        echo "We have a 0";
        break;
    case 1:
        echo "We have a 1";
        break;
    case 2:
        echo "we have a 2";
        break;
    default:
        echo "The number doesn't matter";
}
```

With a *switch* statement, a value is checked against cases. If none are found and a default case exists, then this acts similar to our *else* statement found earlier. If certain cases need to have similar actions performed, we can allow actions to fall through to the next case by removing the *break* statement:

```php
$val = 2;

switch ($val) {
    case 0:
    case 1:
        echo "The value is $val";
        break;
    default:
        echo "The number doesn't matter";
}
```

Sometimes, you may quickly need to save a value from a condition without much fuss. In this case, you may want to use *ternary operators/logic* (?:). The format is simple:

```php
$val = ((condition) ? (true) : (false));
# $val will equal either true or false,
# depending on the conditional result.
```

Now let's look at a real example:

```php
$v1 = 1;
$v2 = 2;

$v1_Greater = ($v1 > $v2 ? true : false);
# $v1_Greater will be false.
```

You're not limited to boolean return values and can return whatever you need. This is merely shorthand to quickly get a value.

Flow control is extremely useful, but sometimes it's not enough on its own. Say, for example, you have PHP connect to a database and output what it finds. The problem is that it finds 5,000 rows of information and hardcoding variables by hand will take you an unreasonable amount of time. This is where *looping* comes in. The looping structures that we will cover in this chapter are *for, while, do while,* and *foreach*. No one loop structure is better than the other, as each is useful under certain circumstances.

As always, let's begin by dissecting some sample code using the *for* loop:

```php
$arr = array(1, 2, 3);

# Grab the size of the array.
# ('sizeOf' explained later)
$arrCount = sizeOf($arr);

for ($i = 0; $i < $arrCount; $i++) {
    # Output each value to the screen.
    echo "Value is " . $arr[$i] . "\n";
}

/* At the end we see:
 * Value is 1
 * Value is 2
 * Value is 3
 */
```

First, we define our $arr variable and assign the values *1, 2,* and *3* (at the default index 0, 1, 2). Next, we grab the size of the array via PHP's *sizeOf* function (explained later) and save the value to $arrCount. Our *for* loop is next, which generally runs three commands:

1. Create and/or assign a starting value to a variable to begin the loop ($i = 0).
2. For each iteration of the loop, run a check (is the value of $i less than the value of $arrCount?).
3. After running the commands inside the for loop, increment the counter ($i++).

Everything within the curly braces will be executed when the loop runs. If no curly braces are defined, the next statement following the loop will be considered part of the loop, and that's it. The variable *$i* is a very popular variable name for traversing a loop and you'll see it used often in other scripts across the web. We use it in this loop to walk us through the array and output the value of the variable at the parallel point of the array.

Another type of loop is the *while* loop. The *while* loop will run as long as the condition that it is checking is satisfied. Poorly coded *while* loops can potentially run forever, so be careful. Let's take a look at some sample code:

```php
$var = true;
$count = 0;
while ($var) {
    echo "We're at loop number ".$count++;
    if ($count > 5) {
        $var = false;
    }
}
```

You're not required to set any values outside of the while loop, but since a while loop will only run if its condition is met, we set our $var to true and created a counter to follow our progress. Next, we output the loop number we were passing through and incremented the $count variable on the same line (post-incrementation). We only wanted the loop to run a handful of times, so we set up an if statement to check our counter and assign $var to false. Once the loop completes and sees that $var is no longer true, we exit the loop.

Almost exactly identical to the *while* loop is the *do while* loop. The only difference between the two is that the *do while* loop will always execute at least on the first pass, regardless of the condition:

```php
$var = false;

do {
    echo "We're in the loop!\n";
} while ($var);

# Outputs one time:
# We're in the loop!
```

Even though $var is false, the loop still runs the first time, then exits when it sees that the condition is not met to continue on.

Even though we can use a *for* loop to traverse an array using the $i variable, PHP gives us a much simpler way using the *foreach* loop. Let's look at some sample code:

```php
$arr = array(1, 2, 3);

foreach ($arr as $value) {
    echo "Our value is $value\n";
}

/* Outputs:
 * Our value is 1
 * Our value is 2
 * Our value is 3
 */
```

After we define an array with values, we pass the array
to our foreach loop, use the *as* keyword to tell the loop
to walk us through the array expressing each value as
our specified variable name (in this case, $value).
$value becomes a copy of the original value and let's us
easily access it via our foreach loop. There are times
when we may need more detailed information, such as
knowing which index we're at in the array. We can also
assign a key variable which will hold our index. Let's
look at the same loop, but saving a key:

```php
$arr = array(1, 2, 3);

foreach ($arr as $key => $value) {
    echo "Our key is $key and";
    echo " our value is $value\n";
}

/* Outputs:
 * Our key is 0 and our value is 1
 * Our key is 1 and our value is 2
 * Our key is 2 and our value is 3
 */
```

You may also want to set a value within the foreach loop, but remember that the value is copied so changing the value of $value isn't the way to go. If you set a key variable, you can directly manipulate the array:

```
$arr = array(1, 2, 3);

foreach ($arr as $key => $value) {
    $arr[$key] = 0;
}

# $arr now has 0 in all fields.
```

You may notice that we didn't use $value anywhere in the above example, but it doesn't matter (only use what you need). Also, the key does not need to be named $key, nor does the value need to be named $value. They can be named whatever you want, but make sure that you use descriptive keywords.

The final things to show you about looping is that you can stop the loop before it would normally end (*break*) and you can skip over portions of code (*continue*):

```
$arr = array(1, 2, 3);

@foreach ($arr as $key => $value) {
    if ($key == 0) {
        continue;
    } else if ($key > 1) {
        break;
    }
    $arr[$key] = 0;
}
```

Once we're in the foreach loop, we check to see if we're at index 0 of our array. If we are, we don't want to proceed for this run and we want to continue to the next iteration. Otherwise, if our key is greater than 1, we want to go ahead and jump out of the loop altogether. If none of the conditions are met, set the array element to 0. In our case, only $array[1] will be set to 0 and the rest of the elements will remain unaffected. You may have noticed that the foreach loop had an *at sign* (@) in front of this. A foreach loop should only be run on an array, otherwise it will produce a warning. To supress any type of warning, you can place the at sign in front of your code. This is not the best way to do it, but it's shown here because you're bound to see it in code that you come across. The best thing to do would be to check if you have an array and only run the foreach loop in that scenario, or to cast the variable to an array if it is not. Though we've already covered casting variables, we'll look at functions to check what variable types we have in the next chapter.

Looping is an extremely powerful control structure. When coupled with flow control, you can get your code to do anything that you need. Just remember that all loops should be surrounded by curly braces. That little tip can save you hours in debugging time.

6 FUNCTIONS

As you saw in the last chapter, control structures like loops allow a lot of work to be done with just a little bit of code. *Functions* are another structure that allow us a lot of flexibility. Functions are blocks of statements that can be used over and over again in your scripts. PHP has a ton of them built in, which are extremely well documented on their site, but you may also create your own functions. Let's create a function and take a look at it:

```php
<?php

function myFunc()
{
    # Code goes here.
}

?>
```

We start by defining our function with the keyword *function,* then we use a name that is not a reserved keyword (like *while* or *function)* and a function name that has not been used before. Function names are **not** case sensitive (*myFunc* is the same as *MYFUNC*) and they may share a name with a variable, but there are still best practices to follow. Stick with the camel case naming convention and give functions and variables different names so that you can easily tell them apart.

Defining a function does not call it or execute any of its code. To do so, you must call the function explicitly:

```php
<?php

echo "I'm outside of the function.";
myFunc();

function myFunc()
{
    echo "Now I'm inside the function.";
}

# Outputs: I'm outside of the function
# Now I'm inside of the function.

?>
```

After the script runs, you'll see *I'm outside of the function* and then you'll see *Now I'm inside of the function* output. You may call a function anywhere and as many times as you need, though we've only called it once in the example. It isn't necessary to define a function before calling it, but it needs to be defined somewhere in your linked code.

When defining your own functions, it's important to understand a boundary called *variable scope.* Variables that are outside of your function are not normally accessible inside of your function:

```php
<?php

$var = 5;
echo $var;
# Outputs the number 5.

addNum();
# Outputs the number 1.

echo $var;
# Outputs the number 5.

function addNum()
{
    # Add one first, then echo.
    echo ++$var;
}

?>
```

The output here is **5**, then **1**, then **5** again. Let's figure out why. You'll notice that $var is set to 5, then the addNum function is called. However, since $var is no longer in scope, it is null when referenced inside of the addNum function. $var wasn't destroyed, but $var within the function is seen as a completely different variable. Think of it like the function is a city and the variable is a person. Somebody named Bob that lives in Los Angeles is not the same person as somebody else named Bob that lives in Houston, even though they share the same name. Once we leave the function, $var inside is gone and we output our original $var value of 5.

You may be thinking *if nothing is in scope within a function, how are any values ever passed to them?* The answer is that there are 4 ways:

1. Pass by value.
2. Pass by reference.
3. Default values.
4. Global variables (not recommended)

We call values that are passed to a function *arguments* or *parameters*. Passing *by value* makes a copy of your variable, then passes it to the function. The original remains untouched. Any transformations done while inside the function **will not** affect the original value. Passing *by reference* passes the original value to your functions. Changes made to the value inside of the function **will** affect the original value. *Default values* are used when values are not set for any and all arguments. This means that if you don't pass the function a value, it will use the default one. The last way is to use *global variables.* Global variables allow varying scope depending on how they're called, but are not considered best practice because they don't adhere to the principle of *high cohesion and low coupling.* This simply means that it's best to keep segments of code (like functions) completely separate. Otherwise, if there is ever a need to change or remove a function later, it is much more likely to break your script's functionality. Let's look at an example which uses all of these methods:

```php
<?php

$var = 5;

addByVal($var);
# $var is still 5.

addByRef($var);
# $var is now 6.

addByDefault();
# $var is still 6.

addByGlobal();
# $var is now 7.

function addByVal($var)
{
    $var++;
    # $var is now 6, but
    # only within this function.
}

function addByRef(&$var)
{
    $var++;
    # $var is now 6 and will persist
    # outside of this function.
}

function AddByDefault($var = 5)
{
    # Default value of 5 is used
    # only when not passed in.
```

```
    $var++;
    # $var loses scope when this
    # function ends.
}




function addByGlobal()
{
    global $var;
    $var++;
}

?>
```

We start by assiging 5 to $var before running through
any functions. The *addByVal* function takes $var as an
argument (passed by value) and adds 1 to $var.
However, this value loses scope once the function ends
and the value outside of the function remains untouched
and is still 5. Next, the *addByRef* function takes $var as
an argument (passed by reference) and adds 1 to $var.
Since this value is passed by reference, which is denoted
by prepending an ampersand to our variable name in the
function declaration, the changes made to $var persist
after the function has ended. Next, the *addByDefault*
function is given no parameters and instead uses the
default value that is assigned when no value is passed in
its place. This ends up working the same as when
passed by value. Lastly, the *addByGlobal* function is
called and takes no arguments. However, once we're
inside the function declaration, we use the keyword
global to let our script know that we want to reference
the original $var variable. This has the same effect as

passing by reference, but has made our code less modular since it depends much more on values outside of its normal scope.

You are not limited to sending one argument at a time to a function, so long as the function is written to handle them. When allowed, they may be sent in comma delimited form:

```php
function myFunc($a, $b, $c)
{
    # Code goes here...
}
```

You may also name the values whatever you like in the function declaration, so long as they're in order. It does not matter what they were named before they were passed in:

```php
$var1 = 1;
$var2 = 2;

myFunc($var1, $var2);
# Outputs 3

function myFunc($x, $y)
{
    $total = $x + $y;
    echo $total;
}
```

Default values work very well when you only want to send a certain number of arguments. However, it's important to remember that you must send the arguments in the correct order that they're defined:

```
myFunc(5);
# Outputs 5.

myFunc();
# Outputs 0.

myFunc(2, 2);
# Outputs 4.
function myFunc($a = 0, $b = 0)
{
    $total = $a + $b;
    echo $total;
}
```

During the first run, we only send one argument. The function then uses the default value of 0 for the second argument and adds them together. During the second function call, we send no arguments and use the default values for both. On the last function call, since we sent our own arguments, we don't use the default values at all. Once we get into PHP's built in function set, you'll find that it's extremely common to rely on default arguments to save having to type something over and over again.

Being able to pass arguments to a function is useful, but we may also get a function to return us a value (which makes keeping code separate much easier).

Just as in mathematics, a function may only return **1** value at most. However, that value may be a string, an array (containing many values), an object (covered later), etc. Return statements may appear in multiple places within your script, but when the script is executed, anything past the return statement will not be run. In later examples we'll look at how it's used in conjunction with flow control, but for now let's look at some of PHP's built in functions.

Func_get_args is a great built in function that returns us with an array of all of the arguments passed in and their values. Let's take a look at how it works:

```php
<?php

$total = addNums(1, 2, 3);
echo "Our total is $total";

function addNums($x, $y, $z)
{
    $total = 0;
    foreach (func_get_args() as $value) {
        $total += $value;
    }
    return $total;
}

?>
```

Now that our function has a return value, we can easily save it. Three numbers are passed to our *addNums* function and saved as $total. Within the function, we use the return value from *func_get_args* that returns an array with all of our arguments as values. Since foreach loops can easily walk through arrays, we run through it and add each value to our total. This total is returned at the end of the function.

You may be wondering how we know that *func_get_args* even exists since it's not defined anywhere in our script. PHP has one of the best documentation libraries online that I've ever seen. Before you create your own function, run your desired functionality through any search engine to see if one already exists in PHP. In fact, go to a search engine right now and type in "**php get function arguments**" . The first page that came up was the php.net site with the function completely documented:

http://php.net/func_get_args

Here we see that the function takes no arguments and returns an array *in which each element is a copy of the corresponding member of the current user-defined function's argument list.* After a little trial and error, you can get many of these built in functions to do exactly what you need.

Functions can only return one value and anything after a return statement will not be executed, but you're likely to see multiple return statements in code that you come across. That may seem contradictory, but flow control can actually make this very useful:

```php
<?php

$var1 = 1;
$var2 = 2;

if (valsAreEqual($var1, $var2)) {
    echo "They are equal";
} else {
    echo "They are NOT equal";
```

```
}

function valsAreEqual($a = NULL, $b =
NULL)
{
    # Check for null values.
    foreach (func_get_args() as $value) {
        if (is_null($value)) {
            return false;
        }
    }

    if ($a == $b) {
        return true;
    } else {
        return false;
    }
}

?>
```

Make sure that you notice that our if statement is
evaluating the return value of the *valsAreEqual* function
that we created. There is no requirement that you save
the return value of a function to a variable , and you
should only do it when it makes sense (such as for
readability). Our function has the default argument
values, but in our case they're not needed since we pass
in our own 2 arguments. The function checks, via the
foreach loop, to make sure that values were actually
passed in. *Is_null* is a built in PHP function that is
documented on their site. It simply checks if a value is
null or not and returns a true or false, respectively.
You'll notice that there are return values all over the
function, but they're all nested within different sets of

flow control. This way, if the condition is not satisfied, the return statement is never executed.

All of the examples shown so far have been self-inclusive scripts. This simply means that the entire script has been within one file, which is itself. However, sometimes it's necessary or best to keep files separate and only include them when they're needed (like a separate file for all of your functions). This also makes it easier to share functionality between different scripts. We'll run through the four types that you're likely to encounter and their differences:

1. require()
2. require_once()
3. include()
4. include_once()

All of the require/include types take a file name as an argument, which will generally include the full path to the file name. *Require()* and *require_once()* will issue a fatal error (E_COMPILE_ERROR) when the file can't be found/included, which will halt the script. *Include()* and *include_once()* will only issue a warning (E_WARNING) when the file can't be found/included, and the script will continue running. While the script will continue to run using include, that doesn't mean it will work. You generally want to include essential files with a require and not-so-essential files with an include. Not-so-essential files are usually only something that will affect the look, but not functionality, whereas essential files will be the main engine itself. The difference between using the functions with _once tied to them is that there is an extra check performed within the function to make sure that the code has not already been included (slightly slower due to the check). Properly written code should never have to depend on _once to be added, but we're all human and mistakes do happen. These tools exists for a reason, so use what suits you best. Let's take a look at how to use them:

```php
<?php

# We need our functions.
require("coreFunctions.php");

# For looks only:
include("pageLayout.php");

/*
 * Both of our files, if successfully added,
 * can now be referenced within this script.
 *
 * It's as though they were
 * directly written in here.
 */

?>
```

Although we have variable types that can hold our values, sometimes something a little bolder and static should be used to hold a value. Looking at our earlier example with require/include, while a variable can be used to hold any file path, you may also use a *constant*. Constants are just what they sound like. They are constant values that are not variable, so they should never change. Let's assume that we do not work out of our root directory, but we know what the path name to all of our scripts will be. We can define a constant to hold our value, then just include it every time that we need it:

```php
<?php

define(SCRIPTDIR, "/path/to/directory/");
include(SCRIPTDIR . "myfile.php");

# Translates to:
# /path/to/directory/myfile.php

?>
```

Now, if we ever need to update the path, we only have to update our constant. SCRIPTDIR is all in uppercase, which makes it easier to spot constants from a glance. It is not required to be in uppercase, but it is a good practice.

A common situation that you'll encounter is trying to see if an exact word or pattern is in a string. If you know the exact string that you're looking for, then the *strpos()* function is your best bet:

```php
<?php

$haystack = "This is the string to search";
$needle = "This";

// Check if $needle is in $haystack.
if (strpos($haystack, $needle)) {
    echo "$needle was found!";
} else {
```

```php
    echo "$needle was NOT found!";
}

# Undesired output.
# Outputs: This was NOT found!

?>
```

The first argument for strpos() is the *haystack* that we're searching. The second argument is the *needle* that we want to search for in our haystack. A third, optional and not shown, argument can be an offset from the beginning of the string that you would like to skip over. The return value of strpos() is the numeric position of the **first** occurrence of your needle in the haystack. When strpos() fails to find the string, it will return false. However, since the first occurrence of the string is at position 0, PHP will interpret this to evaluate our 0 to false. So our script will output *This was NOT found!* There is a way to fix this and it requires us checking if the return value is identical to false (use ===):

```php
<?php

$haystack = "This is the string to search";
$needle = "This";

// Check if $needle is in $haystack.
if (strpos($haystack, $needle) !== false)
{
    echo "$needle was found!";
} else {
    echo "$needle was NOT found!";
}
```

```
# Correct output.
# Outputs: This was found!

?>
```

Make sure that you check if the return value is identical (!==) and not just equal to (!=). Since strpos() is case-sensitive when searching, stripos() allows for case-insensitive searches. Other strpos()-like functions exist for different types of usage, like reverse searching.

Sometimes, searching for a single phrase isn't possible. Have you ever tried to enter your email address into a form somewhere and when you submitted it, you were told that your email address was not in the correct format? The script was probably using something called *regular expressions* to see if your email address was in the correct format. Regular expressions search for patterns, rather than exact phrases. If you can effectively get away without using regular expressions and can instead use strpos(), you definitely should. There is overhead involved with regular expressions and also a complication of code. Keep things as simple as you possibly can. Let's take a look at how regular expressions look:

```php
<?php

// We only want to match numbers.
$regex = "/\d+/";
$hay = "The numbers are 456";

// Our result will be stored here.
$matches = array();
```

```php
if (preg_match($regex, $hay, $matches)) {
    print_r($matches);
}

?>
```

Perl Compatible Regular Expressions (PCRE) are the most accepted format for PHP, and require delimiters around the pattern that is being searched for. The haystack exists just as a regular string. Our matches will be an array that, using the function *preg_match()*, returns that pattern (if found). Our script produces this result:

```
Array
(
    [0] => 456
)
```

Pattern searching with regular expressions is extremely powerful and will give your scripts a ton of flexibility. We've only scratched the surface on them, but the important part right now is to realize that they exist as a tool. Again, only use them if you need them as there is significant overhead and code complexity added.

The last area of functions that we'll cover in this chapter is regarding arrays. There are a ton of array functions that make dealing with arrays much easier. We'll take a look at a couple of them that work on a basic level:

```php
<?php

$arr = array(1, 2, 3, 4);

$firstValue = array_shift($arr);
$lastValue = array_pop($arr);

echo "firstValue = '$firstValue'\n";
echo "lastValue = '$lastValue'\n";
print_r($arr);

?>
```

First we setup our array with four numeric elements. Then we run the *array_shift()* function, which removes the first value from our array (in this case '1') and leaves our $arr variable with only three elements. The return values of the shift is saved to $firstValue in this case, but it doesn't require assignment to execute (but then the value is lost). *Array_pop()* works in a similar fashion, but instead removes the last array element (in this case '4'). The return value is saved, but like array_shift, does not require assignment to perform its action. On a side note, the opposite of array_shift is *array_unshift()*. By referencing the array, then sending the values to add to the array as arguments, the values are added to the beginning of the array. *Array_push()* is the opposite of array_pop, which works similar to array_unshift, except that the values are added to the end of the array (this was done earlier using open/close square brackets and works the same way).

There are a number of array functions that exist, from sorting, inserting values into specific portions of arrays, returning array keys, etc. As always, if you ever need specific array functionality, make sure that you check online via any search engine for an existing function before creating one.

7 SUPERGLOBALS

Jumping back to global scope, which pertains to variables globally accessible to your script via the global keyword, there are a number of variables that are global by nature. These variables, like all variables, must begin with a dollar sign. Then, they tend to have an underscore and the variable name in all caps (remember that variable names are case sensitive, while function names are not). These types of variables are called *superglobals* and do not require the *global* keyword before them since they're global by default. Superglobals tend to be associate arrays and in most cases already have values assigned to them based on their state and environment:

1. $_SERVER
2. $_GET
3. $_POST
4. $_COOKIE
5. $_REQUEST
6. $_SESSION

7. $GLOBALS

The $_SERVER superglobal contains information about how the server runs and how it was accessed during execution of your script. These values can be copied and/or used within your script:

```php
<?php

$ip = $_SERVER["REMOTE_ADDR"];

echo "SERVER superglobal from '$ip'\n";
print_r($_SERVER);

?>
```

Here we output our message with the ip address of the node (me) that connected and ran our script. *Print_r()* is a built in PHP function that beautifully prints out all elements of our variable, whether our variable is an array, object, or even a string (check PHP.net for function requirements).

This is what is output in my particular situation, but yours will vary slightly:

SERVER superglobal from '127.0.0.1'

```
Array
(
    [DOCUMENT_ROOT] => /home/myDir/
    [GATEWAY_INTERFACE] => CGI/1.1
    [HTTP_CACHE_CONTROL] => no-cache
    [HTTP_CONNECTION] => keep-alive
    [HTTP_DNT] => 1
```

```
[HTTP_HOST] => fortbendhost.com
[HTTP_PRAGMA] => no-cache
[HTTP_USER_AGENT] => Mozilla/5.0
(Windows NT 6.1; WOW64; rv:25.0)
Gecko/20100101 Firefox/25.0
[PATH] => /bin:/usr/bin
[QUERY_STRING] =>
[REDIRECT_STATUS] => 200
[REMOTE_ADDR] => 127.0.0.1
[REQUEST_METHOD] => GET
[REQUEST_URI] => /test.php
[SCRIPT_FILENAME] => /home/myDir/test
[SCRIPT_NAME] => /test
[SERVER_ADDR] => 143.95.95.133
[SERVER_PORT] => 80
[SERVER_PROTOCOL] => HTTP/1.1
[SERVER_SIGNATURE] =>
[PHP_SELF] => /test
[REQUEST_TIME] => 1386465178
[argv] => Array
    (
    )

[argc] => 0
)
```

The $_GET and $_POST superglobals are usually
populated when an html form is filled out. If you've ever
visited a website before and noticed a very long address
with a question mark, followed by name/value pairs,
then you've probably seen a query string:

http://FortBendHost.com/test.php**?fname=Nick**

The type of arguments seen in the query string populate the $_GET superglobal, via the GET request. If nothing is passed in, then the superglobal array remains empty. Let's look at the request again:

http://fortbendhost.com/test.php?
fname=Nick&lname=Mendoza

```php
<?php

$name = "";
foreach ($_GET as $value) {
    $name .= $value . " ";
}
$name = trim($name);

echo "Name = '$name'\n";
// Output will be:
// Name = 'Nick Mendoza'

?>
```

The $_POST superglobal is populated in a similar fashion, but information is sent via a POST request and is not as easily visible. Using *wget*, a tool independent of PHP, I'll make the post request:

wget --post-data "fname=Nick&lname=Mendoza" http://FortBendHost.com/test.php

The output ends up being the same as our GET request, after we modify our script:

```php
<?php

$name = "";
foreach ($_POST as $value) {
    $name .= $value . " ";
}
$name = trim($name);

echo "Name = '$name'\n";
// Output will be:
// Name = 'Nick Mendoza'

?>
```

After setting cookies (using the *setcookie()* function) the $_COOKIE superglobal contains our stored cookie values. Have you ever clicked a checkbox at a login area that said "remember me"? That was probably handled via a cookie. Cookies are used to identifiy users by placing a small file on the user's computer, which persists far longer than a session (covered later). They can store anything from an email address to user settings. Let's take a look at how to set a cookie:

```php
<?php
// 3600 is 1 hour.
$expire = time() + 3600 * 24;
// Associative array key.
$name = "name";
// Cookie value.
$value = "Nick";

setcookie($name, $value, $expire);
print_r($_COOKIE);
```

```
?>
```

First we set our expiration time to be 1 day. Then we set the key name for our $_COOKIE superglobal and then we set the value that we would like to store. All of this is then stored using the setcookie() function. When accessed via a browser, our cookie value will be displayed:

```
Array
(
    [name] => Nick
)
```

It is important to note that the setcookie() function can only be called before the visitor's headers close and cookies are only normally set when accessing your script via a web browser (not on the command line).

Since you've already seen the way other superglobals work, the $_REQUEST superglobal won't really be anything new. It is simply a combination of the $_GET, $_POST, and $_COOKIE superglobals all copied into one array. It is accessed just as the other ones are.

The $_SESSION superglobal is similar to the $_COOKIE superglobal, but instead of storing a file on the user's computer, a flat file is temporarily stored with the user's information on the server itself and everything is tied together via a session id. This is how you call and set a session:

```php
<?php

// Starts the session.
// Must call before headers close.
session_start();

$_SESSION["madeUpVal"] = "Hello";
/*
 * $_SESSION["madeUpVal"] will be
 * available to us the next time that
 * our script runs, so long as we
 * begin our script with session_start()
 */

print_r($_SESSION);

?>
```

Session_start() **must** be called **before** the visitor's headers close, just like our setcookie() function. If you even echo a single whitespace, the headers will already have closed and your session will not start. In our case, we start the session then assign a string value to a *madeUpVal* $_SESSION element that we create. This is what is output:

```
Array
(
    [madeUpVal] => Hello
)
```

The great thing is that any other time that we need our session variables, we can simply start our session (session_start()) and call what we need. Let's modify

our script now, on the same server:

```php
<?php

// Starts the session.
// Must call before headers close.
Session_start();

print_r($_SESSION);

?>
```

Our output remains the same when we reload the page:

```
Array
(
    [madeUpVal] => Hello
)
```

Sessions make it possible to maintain state in a stateless environment, like the Internet. It allows you to remain logged into sites, without having to log in each time you visit a different portion of the site.

The last superglobal that we're going to take a look at is $GLOBALS. Make sure to notice that there is no underscore between the dollar sign and the name, compared to other superglobals we've covered this chapter. $GLOBALS is an associative array that can store all of the global variables that are used. It's a lot better than using the global keyword to prefix a variable, because having a value like $GLOBALS["myVar"] is much easier to spot than following the trail of breadcrumbs back to a variable's declaration. Let's take a look at how it works:

```php
<?php

$GLOBALS["MadeUpByNick"] = "some text";
myFunc();

function myFunc()
{
    echo "Here is ";
    echo $GLOBALS["MadeUpByNick"];
    # Outputs 'Here is some text'.
}

?>
```

You can also call the print_r() function anytime that you want to see everything that's in the $GLOBALS superglobal array.

Hopefully, now you've seen how useful superglobals can be. Don't let them confuse you, as they're simply arrays available to you anywhere in your script. They all have certain quirks to them, but once you get to using them, it'll be like second nature to you.

8 OBJECT ORIENTED PROGRAMMING

Everything that you've seen so far follows what is called a *procedural programming pattern.* With procedural programming, most of the heaving lifting is done by functions to handle the flow of the script. You walk through the script and reuse code when possible. Nowadays, the most popular programming method is *object oriented programming,* otherwise known as *OOP.* Object oriented programming follows certain design patterns, mainly centered around classes (which are the foundation of objects) and encapsulation (information hiding).

Let's start by figuring out what a *class* is. Think of a class as a blueprint. A healthy human being has a blueprint for how their brain functions, the location of body parts, and how their central nervous system works (among many other things). An *object* is simply a real representation of that class. Sticking with our human example, an object of a class type **human** would be a real person (like you or myself). Nick (me) would be an object of the human class.

Using object oriented programming, it's important to limit how much access you want or need a class to allow. The object Nick (me) of class type **human** does not work at a bank. Since I don't work at a bank, I don't need to know, or even have access to, bank vault security codes. If somebody were to ask (or torture) me, it's not any information that I could give them since I don't have access. This is known as *data encapsulation* or *information hiding*.

All humans are mammals. However, other animals exist in the world that are mammals, but are not human. Through *class inheritance* the human class would *inherit* from the mammal class when the Nick (me) human object is *instantiated* (created). Our Nick object obviously has mammal traits. We may not want our Nick object to have all of the traits, but we can be more selective in our human class. Class inheritance lets us reuse code, similar to how we did it with functions in our earlier chapter. This way, if we create a wolf class, that class can also inherit from the mammal class and still provide a more refined solution for their definition.

A class may inherit from only one other class, but parent classes (a class that we inherit from) may also inherit from another class. For instance, the human class may inherit from the mammal class, while the mammal class may inherit from the animal class. This is because a human has traits of a mammal, and also has traits of an animal. There is a way to simulate multiple inheritance (where classes can inherit from more than one other class) using interfaces, but generally speaking, a class may only inherit from one other class. Hopefully, this all makes sense, as I've tried to boil the concept of classes and objects down to as little as possible. Let's take a look at some code:

```php
<?php

class human
{
    private $name;

    public function __construct($name)
    {
        // Called during object creation.
        $this->name = $name;
    }

    public function shout()
    {
        echo "My name is " . $this->name;
    }
}

// Instantiate our class object
// (which calls the constructor).
$person = new human("Nick");

$person->shout();
# Outputs: My Name is Nick.

?>
```

We begin by using the *class* keyword, followed by the name of the class that we're creating (whatever name you want), all wrapped in curly braces (like a function). Inside of the class definition, we see a variable name with a *private* keyword before it. Do you remember that earlier in this chapter I was talking about data encapsulation, also known as information hiding? This *private* keyword tells our class that the $name variable is **not** accessible outside of our class. Anything outside of this class that attempts to access or change the value of that variable will fail. Other keywords that you're likely to see are *public* and *protected*. A public variable is accessible anywhere in your script, so long as the class object is in scope. There are no restrictions on public variables. Protected variables are similar to private variables in that they are not accessible outside of their defined class, **however**, any class that inherits from this class **will** have access to that variable. Think of protected variables as being accessible within a class's family only. Next we move onto our *public function __construct()*. The public keyword acts the same for variables as it does for functions, where there are no restrictions on running this function, so long as you're in scope. The function name of *__construct()* is not voluntary, in this case. This is known as a *magic method constructor*. Magic methods are functions that have two underscores (__) prefix the function name and have certain instructions. The constructor is the function that will be run when the class is instantiated (created). Usually you'll want to set the base configuration for your class here. Inside of our constructor, we see a new type of variable. *$this->name* has a few parts to it. *$this* references the object that we're currently in (this object is our current object). The → symbol is the *member access operator*, which consists of a hyphen followed by a right angle bracket. The member access operator allows us to access our variables and functions within our object. From $this object, we want to set the $name variable to whatever was passed in when the object was instantiated. The *public function shout()* does not run when the object is created. It instead runs when it is manually called from outside the script (in this case). After the class definition is exited, we see how our object is created. The class is instantiated by using the *new* keyword, followed by the class name, with the arguments passed in for the constructor. The result is then assigned to our variable ($person). After our $person object is created, with the $name inside set to "Nick", the shout() member function is accessed via our $person object. Do you see why we don't use $this to access our shout() member function? We're no longer referencing $this object anymore. Now we're referencing the $person object.

Generally, you'll want to put your class definitions into separate files from your script. Once inside the script, you would then use the require/include functions to add them. This way, you can use the classes in multiple scripts, but it also makes it easier to find the class later when you need to edit it and have it carryout across any platform where it's used.

You may remember that I made reference to a class being able to inherit from another class. The point of inheritance is to allow your class access to variables (either protected or public) that are within the parent class. This can even include the constructor itself. If you fail to provide a constructor, the class will look to the parent for a constructor and try to run that one. If the parent also does not have a constructor, it will run the *default constructor*, which is simply an empty constructor that does nothing. Let's look at some code:

First we create our file called *class.mammal.php:*

```php
<?php

class mammal
{
    protected $name;

    public function __construct($name)
    {
        $this->name = $name;
    }
}

?>
```

We have a basic class with a protected variable that will be accessible to all children and the class itself. Next we create a file called *class.human.php:*

```php
<?php

require("class.mammal.php");

class human extends mammal
{
    public function shout()
    {
        echo "My name is " . $this->name;
    }
}

?>
```

Within our human class, we reply on the constructor from the mammal class and simply define a shout() member function. From our third script, which we execute, we call each class and reference them:

```php
<?php

require("class.human.php");

$person = new human("Nick");
$person->shout();

?>
```

We get the same result as before, but we've separated all classes into their own files and changed the way that the classes interact together.

As you've seen with functions, classes can save you from a lot of heavy lifting when it comes to being able to reuse code. Classes, however, give you a lot more control over how properties within the class (variables and functions) are hidden from other parts of your script. You're also not restricted to using only functions or classes within your script and object variables (like $person) can be passed to your functions if need be. I've tried to boil down to the basics when it comes to object oriented programming. The goal of this chapter was to get you acquainted with object oriented programming, where extended examples can be seen online:

http://php.net/manual/en/language.oop5.php

9 WHERE TO GO FROM HERE

Have you ever been to a website before and been forced to enter a string of text in the form of random letters and numbers to be able to move to the next screen? Sometimes they're hard to read and offer an audio option if you're unable to make out the text. They're called *CAPTCHAs* and they're meant to make it harder for automated scripts to register accounts and what not. Building your own CAPTCHAs may seem like a difficult task on the surface, but if we look back on what we've learned for far, it's really not all that hard. PHP boils down to the *manipulation of text*. Whether you're doing something simple like searching a string for a word or processing API requests and loading specific objects as a result. The text comes to you in one form or another and you act, with more text, based on that result. However, having an abstract understanding of what's going on is essential.

So looking back on what we've learned so far, we know that we need to have some text persist past one screen. In that case, we need to use our $_SESSION superglobal. We could use $_COOKIES, but the safer bet would be $_SESSION since those are flat files under our control, stored on our server, instead of the user's computer. We can create a $_SESSION["captcha"] variable with a random number generating function, that way it will be a different (random) value each time a user visits our page. By using a search engine, I find that I can use a GD library in PHP to make the image using my $_SESSION["captcha"] variable and a combination of GD functions like imagecreate(), imagecolorallocate(), and imagettftext(). So I pass my $_SESSION["captcha"] value to those functions and have it create my image. When we get to the second part of the script, since our $_SESSION superglobal value is still present, we can check if the text that our site visitor supplied was input correctly.

It's not just about creating everything that you need from scratch, either. If you're a blogger or use WordPress as a CMS (Content Management System) for your website, you have a wealth of code available to you. These functions like get_adjacent_post() or wp_delete_post() are not built into PHP, but instead extend it using its own framework to save you from having to do more heavy lifting than is needed:

http://codex.wordpress.org/Function_Reference

I realize that a lot of this is easier said than done. You're probably a very busy person, either starting/running your own blog and wanting more functionality with WordPress or you're trying to wrap your head around programming and figured that PHP was a good starting point. Whatever your case may be, it's important to understand that *results don't care.* Successful results have requirements that need to be met and no matter how difficult your situation is, success will elude you if you don't make time for it. Even if you simply take your lunch break at work and use that time to read an article on PHP, work through some test code, or even write your own scripts, you will be miles ahead of what most people are willing to do. Over time, that will lead to success. I say none of this to be mean or heartless, but I can't stress enough how important it is to continue learning and applying what you've learned so far. If you take daily action, you will get better, but you've got to do it consistently. If you don't take action, you'll soon begin to forget what you've learned and probably have to start back over again.

You may be wondering, *but where do I go from here?* To make the growth process as easy as possible, I've created a special package for readers of this book. The details are available here:

<u>http://FortBendHost.com/Book-Offer</u>

You'll get PHP setup and configured right out of the box and be able to create a website, a blog, or just make your scripts available to anybody visiting your public site.

The best way to learn something is by actually doing it. Even if you don't sign up for my service, please make sure that you keep learning and practicing. Go on YouTube and watch videos on PHP. Just make sure that you're doing something.

Thank you very much for buying this book and making it to the end. By finishing this book, you've probably already done more than 95% of people that simply want to learn something, but won't make the effort necessary to actually succeed. Thank you again, and please don't stop learning!

ABOUT THE AUTHOR

Nick Mendoza holds a Bachelor of Science Degree in
Computer Science from the California State University
of Fullerton. He works as a software developer,
consultant, and also runs his own webhosting/media
company. When he's not working, he enjoys playing
with video and keeping up with technology.
He lives in a suburb of Houston, Texas, with his wife
and their three dogs.